RACING MANIA

NASCAR

K.C. KELLEY

This edition first published in 2010 in the United States of America
by Marshall Cavendish Benchmark.

Marshall Cavendish Benchmark
99 White Plains Road
Tarrytown, NY 10591-5502
www.marshallcavendish.us

Library of Congress Cataloging-in-Publication Data
Kelley, K.C.
NASCAR / by K.C. Kelley.
p. cm. — (Racing mania)
Summary: "Provides comprehensive information on the history, the famous faces, the design,
and the performance of the amazing machines behind NASCAR"–Provided by publisher.
Includes bibliographical references and index.
ISBN 978-0-7614-4387-2
1. Stock car racing—United States—Juvenile literature.
2. NASCAR (Association)—Juvenile literature.
I. Title.
GV1029.9.S74K4543 2010
796.72–dc22
2009004498

Cover: Joe Robbins
Half Title: Joe Robbins
p4: Auto Imagery Inc.; P5: Joe Robbins; P6: Bettmann/Corbis; p7: Getty Images;
p8: Focus on Sport/Getty Images; p9: Joe Robbins; pp10-11: Bettmann/Corbis;
p11: RacingOne/Getty Images; pp12-13: Getty Images Sport/Getty Images; p13: RacingOne/
Getty Images; p14: Sports Illustrated/Getty Images; p15: Focus on Sport/Getty Images;
p16-17: Focus on Sport/Getty Images; p17: John Bazemore/Associated Press; p18: Joe Robbins;
p19: Joe Robbins; p20: Joe Robbins; pp20-21: Auto Imagery Inc.; pp22-23: Auto Imagery Inc.;
pp24-25: Associated Press; p26: Jamie Squire/Getty Images; p27: Auto Imagery Inc.; p28: Auto Imagery
Inc.; p29: Auto Imagery Inc.; p30: Streeter Lecka/Getty Images; p31tr: Adam Pretty/Aus /Allsport/Getty
Images; p31bl: Auto Imagery Inc.; pp32-33: Auto Imagery Inc.; p34: Joe Robbins; p35: Jamie Squire/Getty
Images; p36: Auto Imagery Inc.; p37: Joe Robbins; p38: Joe Robbins; p39: Joe Robbins; p40: Auto Imagery
Inc.; pp40-41: Shutterstock; p42: Auto Imagery Inc.; p43: Joe Robbins; pp44-45: Joe Robbins.

Created by Q2AMedia
Editor: Denise Pangia
Series Editor: Jim Buckley
Art Director: Sumit Charles
Client Service Manager: Santosh Vasudevan
Project Manager: Shekhar Kapur
Designer: Joita Das and Prashant Kumar
Photo research: Shreya Sharma

Printed in Malaysia

1 3 5 6 4 2

CONTENTS

A LOOK AT NASCAR 4

BIRTH OF NASCAR 6

NASCAR IN THE 1960S 8

NASCAR IN THE 1970S 10

THE KING: RICHARD PETTY 12

NASCAR IN THE 1980S 14

NASCAR IN THE 1990S 16

THE MAN IN BLACK: DALE EARNHARDT SR. 18

TODAY'S NASCAR 20

THE CAR OF TOMORROW 22

NASCAR ENGINES 26

TIRES 28

DRIVER GEAR 30

PIT CREW 32

TRACKS 34

RACING STRATEGIES 36

JEFF GORDON 38

OTHER NASCAR STARS 40

JIMMIE JOHNSON 44

GLOSSARY 46

FIND OUT MORE 47

INDEX 48

A LOOK AT NASCAR

Stock car racing has become America's favorite motor sport!

The engines are roaring. The high-tech racing machines zoom around the track at nearly 200 miles per hour (322 kilometers per hour). They are just inches away from one another! The cars bump and crunch as they try to pass one another. Each car aims to grab every bit of speed it can. The fans in the packed stands scream for their favorites as the checkered flag drops. One lucky winner roars across the finish line!

Fans love the tight-packed racing action at a NASCAR race. Forty-three cars start each race. They line up in twenty-two rows of two cars each, with one car at the back of the pack.

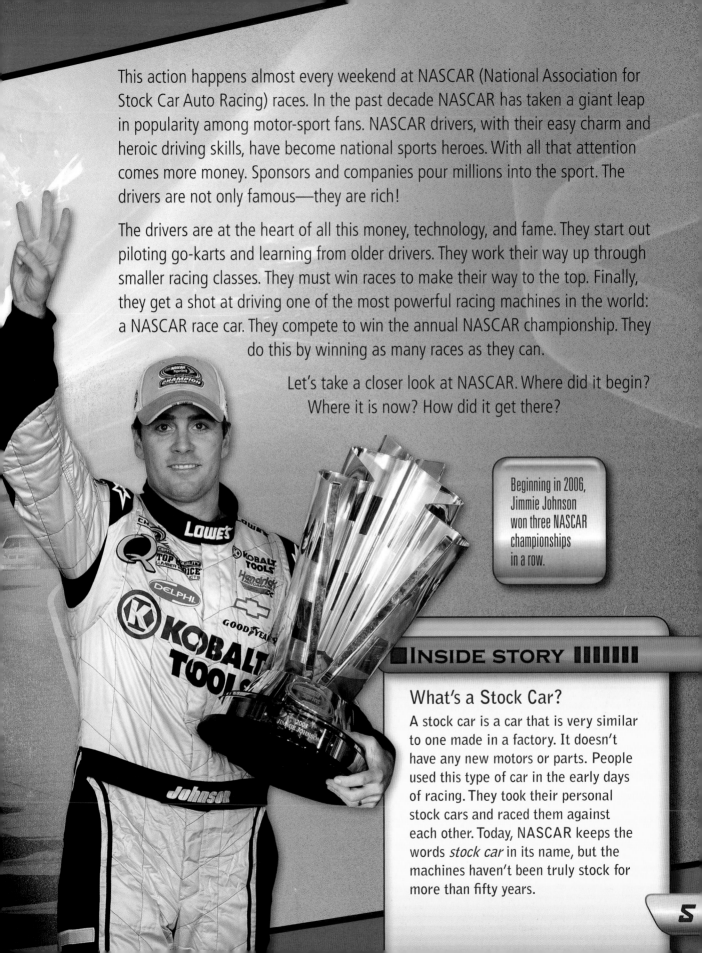

This action happens almost every weekend at NASCAR (National Association for Stock Car Auto Racing) races. In the past decade NASCAR has taken a giant leap in popularity among motor-sport fans. NASCAR drivers, with their easy charm and heroic driving skills, have become national sports heroes. With all that attention comes more money. Sponsors and companies pour millions into the sport. The drivers are not only famous—they are rich!

The drivers are at the heart of all this money, technology, and fame. They start out piloting go-karts and learning from older drivers. They work their way up through smaller racing classes. They must win races to make their way to the top. Finally, they get a shot at driving one of the most powerful racing machines in the world: a NASCAR race car. They compete to win the annual NASCAR championship. They do this by winning as many races as they can.

Let's take a closer look at NASCAR. Where did it begin? Where it is now? How did it get there?

Beginning in 2006, Jimmie Johnson won three NASCAR championships in a row.

▌INSIDE STORY ▐▐▐▐▐▐

What's a Stock Car?

A stock car is a car that is very similar to one made in a factory. It doesn't have any new motors or parts. People used this type of car in the early days of racing. They took their personal stock cars and raced them against each other. Today, NASCAR keeps the words *stock car* in its name, but the machines haven't been truly stock for more than fifty years.

NASCAR started after outlaw drivers looked for ways to drive more often and more safely.

Car lovers have always raced cars! In the 1920s one of the hottest areas of the country for fast cars was in the southern United States. Laws passed in 1919 made the selling of liquor illegal, but people still wanted to drink it. Those who wanted to avoid this law hired people to drive fast cars through the countryside delivering illegal liquor. The laws changed eventually, but those drivers still wanted to go fast. So they raced.

People in the 1920s made illegal liquor in machines like these, called stills. Fast drivers then delivered the cargo to customers.

They were driving cars that had not been fitted out especially for racing. These were just stock cars. The drivers made them special. Over the years more drivers wanted to match their skills with other speed demons. In the late 1940s a group of drivers decided to band together to create better racing conditions.

The leader of this group was "Big" Bill France Sr., a driver from Florida. He felt drivers should work together so they could command more money from track owners. This would also attract new sponsors and ensure safe, fair races. The drivers would have more control. France formed NASCAR in 1948, and the France family has run it ever since. In 1971, Bill's son, Bill Jr., took over, and then his grandson, Brian. Brian France is the leader of today's NASCAR.

A pair of NASCAR legends battle in this 1960 race. Junior Johnson (27) slides past Curtis Turner (26) as the two cars speed down the track.

In that first decade NASCAR went through many changes. Drivers wanted to **modify** their cars even more. They wanted to turn their everyday cars from stock cars to full-out racing machines. NASCAR guided these changes, making sure they were fair to all. For example, it made sure that cars of the same size raced against each other. The organization's success led to the construction of huge speedways where thousands of fans could watch the races. From a hobby practiced by **gearheads**, stock car racing quickly became a major motor sport.

■ INSIDE STORY ||||||

On the Beach!

One of the most popular places to run early stock car races was on the beach. Daytona Beach, Florida, boasted wide beaches of hard-packed sand. A course was laid out that took drivers along a dirt track, around a curve, and then down the beach. Hundreds of races were held there in all sorts of cars. "Big" Bill France, who would go on to create NASCAR, first laid out the track. Daytona Beach International Speedway, opened in 1959, was the site of the largest hard-track superspeedway.

NASCAR IN THE 1960s

The decade of the 1960s was one of slow and steady growth for NASCAR, and it saw the rise of a legend.

The 1960s were a period of change for NASCAR. The sport grew steadily from a small-time organization in the south to a more national motor sport. More fans were attracted to the sport. New tracks popped up in many places. In the 1950s drivers and their helpers raced in their spare time. Soon more money came into the sport from sponsors. The drivers and teams were able to make NASCAR their daily job.

The cars, too, became better. The stock cars of the past were fading quickly. Vehicles were now built from the start to be racers. The body types were still similar to those

This was one of the cars driven by Richard Petty, who dominated the sport for nearly twenty years, beginning in the mid–1960s.

43

"THE RACER'S EDGE"

David Pearson, known as "The Silver Fox" for his driving tricks, won three NASCAR championships in the late 1960s.

sold as passenger cars. That was important, as the carmakers were big sponsors. Seeing star driver Richard Petty in a Dodge, Plymouth, or Ford might inspire someone to buy one for himself. The idea of "drive on Sunday, buy on Monday" played a big part in NASCAR's rise.

Those high-tech engines also caused problems. NASCAR officials found themselves in a race of their own. Teams and car owners kept trying new and more powerful engines and engine parts. NASCAR had to change its rules often to make sure races were fair. They didn't want one team to have an unfair advantage.

Great drivers emerged among all this new money and new technology. Richard Petty became "The King," but there were other stars. Joe Weatherly won the championship in 1962 and 1963. The win served as a final nod to the sport's early stars. David Pearson was a three-time champion. Pearson was a link to the early days, too. He took advantage of the great new cars, but he drove as if he was still trading paint with his opponents. This refers to cars scraping off colorful paint jobs when they crashed into one another.

■ INSIDE STORY ||||||

The Hemi Argument

In 1966 Richard Petty tried to make changes to his cars to help him win. This angered a lot of people. His first move was to install a powerful engine called a hemi. His second was to put a raised wing of metal along the back of his car. The air rushing over this wing pushed the car down on the track more firmly. NASCAR soon banned these changes.

NASCAR IN THE 1970s

Big money hit NASCAR for the first time in this decade and the sport took off.

In 1972 NASCAR changed in a major way. Winston, a cigarette company, agreed to become the sport's biggest sponsor. They would pay a huge amount of money. NASCAR used the money to increase the amount of prize money that could be won and to promote the sport. The annual championship became known as the Winston Cup. It was a big deal and NASCAR leaped ahead. By the middle of the decade, attendance at NASCAR races topped one million for the first time.

Some races were shown on television. This expanded the audience for the sport. By 1979 the Daytona 500 was on national TV for the first time. Detroit, home to many race cars used in NASCAR, added a track.

In the 1970s, NASCAR race cars looked very much like the cars people drove every day.

Janet Guthrie was a pioneer racer. She was the first woman in the Daytona 500.

The 1970s were a decade in which women began to play a bigger role in many parts of American life. NASCAR got its first woman driver (some women had raced stock cars in the 1940s), Janet Guthrie, who qualified and competed in the Daytona 500 in 1977. She finished twelfth. No other women have raced at NASCAR's top level since. Though the sport was growing nationally, southern drivers were still among the regular winners. North Carolina's Richard Petty and South Carolina's Cale Yarborough won eight of the championships in the decade. The Alabama Gang was a group of winning drivers from that state. This included brothers Donnie and Bobby Allison, Bobby's son Davey, and Neil Bonnett.

NASCAR was moving forward fast and would just keep getting bigger.

■ INSIDE STORY ⅠⅠⅠⅠⅠⅠ

Cale Yarborough

Before Jimmie Johnson matched him in 2008, Cale Yarborough was the only driver ever to capture three straight NASCAR championships. Yarborough had a long and successful driving career starting in 1957. He roared to the top in the 1970s, winning NASCAR titles in 1976, 1977, and 1978. His eighty-three race wins make him third in the all-time list of race winners.

THE KING: RICHARD PETTY

More than a quarter century after his last race, Richard "The King" Petty remains NASCAR's greatest all-time champ.

Richard Petty became a racer by following in his father's tire tracks. Lee Petty won three NASCAR championships and the first Daytona 500 in 1959. By that year his son Richard had moved from a job in his father's mechanic shop to a spot behind the wheel. Soon, young Richard was roaring past his dad and every other driver in the circuit.

Petty's cars had a famous red-and-blue design, based on his car's sponsor, STP.

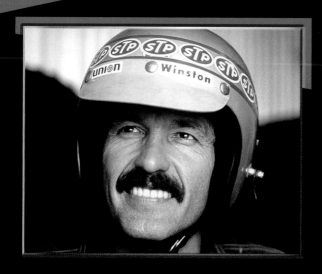

Petty's smiling face has been a part of just about every NASCAR event since he started in 1959.

In 1964 he started out by winning his first Daytona 500. By the end of the season he matched his dad as a NASCAR champion. Petty went on to win six more NASCAR championships. Only Dale Earnhardt Sr. would match Petty's total of seven. Petty also set the career record of 200 race wins. In fact, the driver in second place, David Pearson, has just over half of that total with 105 wins. Petty's greatest year came in 1967. He won ten consecutive races, along with twenty-seven of the season's thirty-eight races.

While Petty won two titles in the 1960s, it was in the 1970s that he was truly dominant. He won five NASCAR titles in the decade. He won his last race in 1984 (the Firecracker 400) and raced for the last time in 1992. His Fan Appreciation Tour attracted millions of fans. Petty has since become a successful race team owner. Together with his son Kyle, Petty runs a series of camps for kids with cancer. For this, and many other reasons, it's no surprise that Richard Petty is known as "The King."

■ INSIDE STORY ||||||

Petty vs. Pearson

A great champion like Petty needs a great rival. He had one in David Pearson. Known as the "Silver Fox," Pearson won 105 races, second only to Petty's 200. They finished first and second in sixty-three races. Pearson actually won three more of those races than "The King." Pearson was also a three-time NASCAR champ in 1966, 1968, and 1969. Their final-lap crash in the 1976 Daytona 500, resulting in a Pearson win, was one of NASCAR's most famous races.

NASCAR IN THE 1980s

A new hero emerged in this decade. Racing got even more technical, and faster.

The addition of TV to the NASCAR mix made the sport even bigger in the 1980s. With the backing of Winston, NASCAR was able to expand and attract even more sponsors. With the growing audience, it meant that TV was ready to come on board in a big way. More races were shown on local or national TV. Sponsors raced to get their names and logos on the cars. For most of the previous years, the sponsors who came to NASCAR were from the automotive industry. They included carmakers, oil producers, and gas companies. With the rise of TV, other products came into the mix. Tide laundry detergent, for instance, was a major sponsor of Darrell Waltrip, who won three Winston Cup championships in the decade.

Rising star Dale Earnhardt Sr. (2) rides the bumper of David Pearson (11). Driving very close to the car in front can help the car behind go very fast with less effort and less gas!

In his familiar sponsor colors, Darrell Waltrip celebrates another win on his way to three titles.

In 1980 Dale Earnhardt Sr., "The Man in Black," won his first championship. He went on to win two more in the 1980s for a total of seven overall, matching Petty. Waltrip took three titles (1981, 1982, and 1985), veteran Bobby Allison won in 1983, and Terry Labonte came in first in 1984.

Labonte's title was significant. He was the last driver in NASCAR history not to reach $1 million in annual earnings. The extra cash from TV, Winston, and other sponsors pushed the top drivers into making the kind of money that had, in the past, only been earned by the top basketball, football, or baseball stars. NASCAR was playing in the big leagues!

■INSIDE STORY ||||||

Elliott's Big Day

In the days before restrictor plates, on-track speeds were creeping up. Engines got more powerful. In a qualifying lap at Talladega International Speedway in 1987, Bill Elliott put together the greatest four laps in history. He drove his Ford Thunderbird to a new all-time record of 212 miles per hour (341 km/h). More than twenty years later, that remains the record for a NASCAR racing machine.

NASCAR IN THE 1990s

New fans and new stars helped NASCAR take even bigger steps forward in the 1990s.

How big did NASCAR get in the 1990s? The overall champion in 1999, Dale Jarrett, took home more than twice as much money ($6.6 million) as the 1990 winner, Dale Earnhardt Sr. ($3 million). Where did all of that money come from? Most of it came from TV.

In 1992 Alan Kulwicki became the last driver/car owner to win the NASCAR championship. The sport had become too expensive for such drivers.

TV networks paid NASCAR more money for the right to put the popular races on the air. NASCAR gave some of that money to the winning drivers. As more and more people watched the races on TV, more sponsors came on board. This added additional money to the winning purses.

Dale Earnhardt Sr. was the top driver of the decade. He won four titles: 1990, 1991, 1993, and 1994. His final championship tied him with Richard Petty for the most titles ever—seven.

Wreck! With cars moving at very high speeds and every driver doing his best to win, accidents (like this one from 1990) happen in NASCAR!

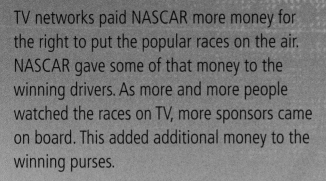

■ INSIDE STORY ||||||

NASCAR Goes to Indy

The Indianapolis Motor Speedway is one of the most famous race tracks in the world. But until 1994, it had never hosted a NASCAR event. Indy was home to the open-wheel Champ Cars. In 1994 NASCAR finally got a crack at the track, with the first running of the Brickyard 400. The name came from Indy's nickname. The original roadway surface was made of bricks. Indiana native Jeff Gordon won the first Brickyard 400.

THE MAN IN BLACK: DALE EARNHARDT Sr.

Black helmet, black shades, black car: Sounds like the villain, right? But NASCAR's "Man in Black" remains one of its most beloved heroes.

Dale Earnhardt Sr. didn't get into racing to make friends. He got into it for only one reason—to win. Few drivers have done so as successfully as Earnhardt, and none with as much intensity and drive.

Earnhardt's father, Ralph, was an early NASCAR driver. Dale Sr. grew up around cars and knew that his destiny was to follow in his dad's path. He got his first full-time ride in a NASCAR car in 1979. The following year he won his first season championship. No other driver had been that good that fast. He moved to a different race team in 1981, getting his famous No. 3 car. From its paint job came his famous nickname: The "Man in Black."

With his dark glasses, thick mustache, and no-nonsense glare, Earnhardt made it clear that he was determined to do anything to win.

Here's a good look at the Chevy Monte Carlo that Earnhardt drove in the 1990s.

eginning in 1986, he dominated NASCAR for a decade. He won six more titles hrough 1994. Earnhardt tried for years to add a Daytona 500 win to his long st of wins, but it took him until 1998 to do it.

hrough it all, Earnhardt earned the love of fans across the country for his no-onsense, bump-and-run style. His personality backed that up with a serious ook at all times. Even after he won, it was odd to see Earnhardt wearing a mile. His other nickname was "The **Intimidator**."

1 2001 there were no smiles. During he Daytona 500 that year, in a race that ncluded his son Dale Jr., an up-and-oming star himself, Earnhardt was near he front of the pack late in the race. uddenly, there was a wreck. Earnhardt yas killed instantly when his car hit a yall. All of NASCAR mourned his death.

o this day, Earnhardt remains one f the most beloved figures in motor oorts, and souvenirs with his famous lo. 3 are still big sellers.

■ INSIDE STORY ||||||

Finally, the 500

Dale Earnhardt Sr. won seven races at the Daytona International Speedway. The trouble was that he never won in February when the famous Daytona 500 is run. Year after year, as great as he was, Earnhardt managed to find a way not to win. He lost when he ran out of gas, or blew a tire, or was passed late in the race. Finally, in 1998, he broke the jinx. After the race, crews from every team lined the pit road to give a high five to one of NASCAR's heroes.

TODAY'S NASCAR

NASCAR is better than ever, with big sponsors, millions of fans, great new cars, and famous drivers!

The biggest change in NASCAR since Winston arrived happened in 2004. That year Winston stopped being NASCAR's top sponsor. The new sponsor was Nextel, which makes cell phones and other gear. Because Winston makes cigarettes, it had been hard to market NASCAR to young people. That's because cigarette companies aren't allowed to advertise on TV. With the new sponsor, NASCAR could go anywhere. Their airtime on TV greatly increased, which was good news to the drivers.

Jimmie Johnson holds up the NASCAR Sprint Cup in 2008.

Another big move was to start a play-off for the championship. For decades the driver with the most points at the end of the season was the champion. Beginning in 2004, NASCAR started the Chase for the Cup. Now, after twenty-six races, the top twelve drivers enter a special play-off over the final ten races. In 2008 the phone company Sprint became the main sponsor. Today, drivers race against each other to win the NASCAR Sprint Cup.

As NASCAR looks ahead, it faces some challenges. In 2008 and 2009 American economic problems caused some sponsors to drop out. Rising fuel prices made it more expensive to run races. Some fans stayed away, too. But stock car racing has been a part of America for sixty years. It's sure to race ahead of the problems!

NASCAR's newest division races super-fast pickup trucks.

▐ INSIDE STORY ▐▐▐▐▐▐

Other Parts of NASCAR

NASCAR's top level is the Sprint Cup for 2009. But NASCAR has other parts. The level of racing below the Sprint Cup is called the Nationwide Series. For many years it was called the Busch Series. Drivers in this series race cars that are slightly slower and larger than Sprint Cup cars. They usually run shorter races on the same tracks as Sprint Cup events, but on weekends. The Craftsman Truck Series is the third NASCAR level. Specially built pickup trucks with enclosed beds zoom around the same tracks as the other levels. Speeds are lower, but the trucks handle differently, so it's a real challenge!

THE CAR OF TOMORROW

In the old days, there were as many different cars in a race as there were drivers. Today all NASCAR teams use the same basic body shape. The two reasons? Fairness and safety.

When NASCAR began, drivers got their race cars from the family garage. Soon they began building their cars from scratch. By the 1960s and 1970s major carmakers were paying to have their cars used in the races. But those cars were only stock on the outside. Inside they were all racing machine. In 2007, for instance, all teams used one of the following car frames: Chevrolet Monte Carlo or Impala; Dodge Intrepid or Avenger; Ford Fusion or Taurus; or Toyota Camry.

In 2008 all NASCAR teams began using the same style: The Car of Tomorrow (COT). After many years of testing, NASCAR came up with this new basic design. The COT means that all teams have a fair shot and can easily follow the rules. Also, the new car is safer for drivers. But, the change didn't happen without some grumbling. Some drivers say that the COT doesn't handle well. Others feel it isn't fast enough. The COT is the law of the land now, and drivers will get used to it.

The wing at the back of the COT helps the car stay on the track more firmly.

The biggest changes are in the driver's compartment, or cockpit, and the rear spoiler, or wing. In the cockpit the driver's seat has been moved slightly toward the center. The wing at the back helps to push the car down on the track. As the air rushes over it, it acts like a reverse airplane wing. While an airplane's wings give lift, the car's wing gives traction.

The COT is also slightly wider and taller than previous models used by teams. Its windshield is a little more upright. These changes help keep the speed of the car down a bit, too. Earlier the cars were getting so fast that NASCAR was afraid drivers would have a harder time staying out of wrecks.

Making the COT is a complicated task. These are the steps that each team goes through to create these amazing racing machines.

1. *Chassis*: The first step is to make the steel skeleton or chassis. Tubes of steel are welded together to form this frame. When it's done, the engine compartment, the cockpit, and the rear area are all visible.

2. *Shell*: The exterior of the car is made of sheets of metal welded together. Special workers called fabricators mold and bend these sheets to create the shape of the body. Having a super-smooth skin on the car is vital to achieving high speed. Any bump or rough spot can slow a car down a fraction. That can make all the difference. For that reason, the shells are carefully joined, polished, and sanded. This creates a smooth skin.

The chassis looks like a steel skeleton. There are places to put the engine (in the front) and for the driver (at back).

Experts attach the metal sheets to the outside of the car (or in this case, the truck).

3. *Systems*: Before the shell is put into place on the chassis, the interior wiring is put in. These cars use thousands of feet of wiring to connect the engine to cockpit systems and other parts of the car. The gas tank is also installed, as well as the driver's control panel. The axles and wheels are put on, too.

4. *Paint*: Just before the shell is put on the chassis, it is painted with special rust-proofing primer. It is then coated with a colorful skin and covered with sponsor stickers.

5. *Engine*: The engine for the car is lowered inside the shell, into the engine compartment. Then, all the connections are made to the rest of the car's systems.

6. *Tires*: The tires are put on last, and then away to the race track!

■INSIDE STORY ||||||

Safer Walls, Too

The COT is designed to protect drivers in new ways. Another safety development is outside the car. In 2003 NASCAR installed a new type of wall called SAFER (steel and foam energy reduction). The walls are softer than concrete and designed to buckle and bend when struck by a car. This spreads out the impact energy, which makes it more likely that the driver will not be hurt. The SAFER walls have saved dozens of drivers from injuries since, and more tracks are installing them.

Mighty engines are the roaring, beating heart of NASCAR racing machines. They're designed to do one thing really well— go fast!

NASCAR works very hard to make sure that every team has a fair shot at winning. This is done by making very specific rules about the engines in the car and what the teams can do to modify them.

NASCAR engines are packed with hundreds of moving parts, all of which must work perfectly.

The main engine can be up to 358 cubic inches (5,867 cubic centimeters). The block, or main part, is made of iron. Most of the other parts are lightweight aluminum. The engines are all V-8, which means they have eight **pistons** churning up and down to power the wheels. They are all limited to 850 horsepower. Compare that to the 200 horsepower your average family sedan can put out!

At super-speedway races, NASCAR engines have to include a special part. The restrictor plate is attached to the top of the carburetor. The carburetor is the part of the engine that mixes gas and air to cause the small explosions that fire the pistons. These pistons move up and down to turn the driveshaft and the wheels. The restrictor plate slightly reduces the amount of air that can get in. This gives the engines less power, which means less speed, and on super-speedways, less speed means more safety.

NASCAR teams actually bring several engines to each race. For the **qualifying** laps, they use a slightly lighter engine because it is needed only for a few laps, and having a lighter engine may mean a tiny bit more speed. The practice engine is then put into the car. During pre-race rehearsal laps, crews fine-tune the engine and the car. Doing this leaves the final, race-day engine fresh for the big event. The night before race, crews install the final, heavy-duty racing engine.

After a race the engine is taken apart, almost piece by piece. It is examined carefully for worn parts. New parts are added and the engine is put back together for the next race.

■INSIDE STORY ▐▌▐▌▐▌

Gas 'Em Up!

The engines are certainly huge and powerful, but they won't go anywhere without fuel. NASCAR engines run on a special high-tech form of gasoline. It is much better than the gasoline you get at your local service station. All the teams must use the same type of gasoline supplied by NASCAR to ensure that teams don't try to use unapproved fuel. Teams refuel the cars during the race with 11-gallon (41.6-liter) cans emptied into the gas tank at the rear of the cars. Special crew members are trained to work with gasoline to prevent accidents.

Expert mechanics carefully check over every part of the engine before the racing starts.

TIRES

They're all round, black, and made of rubber. They all look the same. So why are tires such an important part of a race team's strategy?

With all the attention NASCAR pays to the drivers, engines, and cars, the most important things on the cars are the tires. Race crews spend almost as much time preparing and planning tire use as anything else leading up to a race.

Racing tires have no **tread**. They are flat-surfaced slicks. This tread-free surface helps create a bigger footprint, literally, where the rubber meets the road. This footprint helps give the speeding car good traction on the track. As the heavy cars go through tight turns at high speed, the tires have to grip the road well or else the car can spin.

Race teams keep extra tires stacked near their pit area on the side of the racetrack.

Pit crew members change a car's tires several times during a race to keep the highest speed.

Each race team is supplied with the same tires by Goodyear. This ensures that no team gets an advantage. How each team uses them is the difference. Crews add the amount of air they think will best help their driver control the car or be best for the particular racetrack. During warm-ups and qualifying, they test tires to come up with the best settings for the race. They mark tires carefully so that tire changers will choose the right ones during the race. They might reuse some tires from qualifying to do further tests. To clean off loose bits of rubber, they clean them with a blowtorch.

Tires are attached to the wheels using five lug nuts. To make tire-attaching easier, these lug nuts are lightly glued to the tire so the air gun can grab them and tighten them in a flash. A team might go through a dozen or more sets of tires over a racing weekend.

■INSIDE STORY ▌▌▌▌▌▌▌

Burnout!

Have you ever seen a winning NASCAR driver do donuts on the track after the race? Using the accelerator and brakes, the driver causes the rear tires to spin very fast in place. The friction of rubber on the road creates billowing white smoke as the rubber burns. All that smoke gives the move its name: the burnout. It looks like something is on fire, but really it's just the rubber melting off. And with the race over, they won't need those tires again!

DRIVER GEAR

NASCAR drivers wear everything they can to keep themselves safe and comfortable in their race cars.

When NASCAR started, drivers put on an old pair of jeans and a T-shirt and zoomed off. Some of them even wore helmets! As racing became a big business, teams looked for any edge they could to make their drivers better and safer.

Today's drivers are outfitted head to toe with the latest technology. The helmets are made of Kevlar, the same stuff that's in bulletproof vests. Faceguards are made of shatterproof plastic. Inside the helmets, which are custom-made for each driver, there are systems of tubes that help keep the driver cool. They can even provide the driver with a drink! A radio inside the helmet keeps the driver in touch with the crew back in the pits. Finally, the helmet is attached to the high-tech HANS (Head And Neck Support) device.

This full-body racing suit worn by Matt Kenseth is made of material that is fire resistant.

Moving on to the body, protection against fire is very important. First, drivers put on undergarments that are made of Nomex. This material can keep them—briefly—safe in a fire. Their colorful jumpsuits are also made of fire-retardant materials. They are designed to help keep the drivers cool in the high heat of the driving cockpit. Driving gloves are made of the same material. The gloves are also very flexible to allow the drivers to manage the many controls.

The drivers' feet are also protected from fire. Drivers wear special driving shoes that have a metal plate in the sole. Without that, the rubber on the bottom of the shoe would probably melt after being held on the hot gas and brake pedals for several hours. Many drivers also strap on heel pads made of silver fireproof material. This helps them battle the enormous heat put out by the engine just in front of the driving cockpit.

The silver heel pads help keep a driver's feet cool in the high heat of the cockpit.

■INSIDE STORY ⅠⅠⅠⅠⅠⅠ

Help From HANS

One of the most dangerous parts of a crash is the driver's head whipping suddenly forward or backward. To help prevent that violent motion from harming drivers, they now all use the HANS device. HANS is made of a heavy-duty plastic and metal collar that fits over the driver's shoulders. A cable attached to the back of the driver's helmet keeps the head from whipping around, too. Many experts think that the HANS device has saved many drivers from injury or even death.

PIT CREW

Need gas? Need new tires? You drive to the local garage or gas station. NASCAR drivers head for the pits!

During a race, NASCAR vehicles need help. Just as you would drive your car to a gas station, NASCAR drivers pull over, too. They go to the pits.

Like a squad of buzzing bees, seven pit-crew members leap into action. In fewer than 15 to 20 seconds, they can put 22 gallons (83.3 l) of fuel in the car, change all four tires, and even clean the windshield! If this crew can do its job perfectly, it can mean the difference between winning and losing a race.

The seven crew members who go over the wall each have specific jobs:

1. *Jack Man*: Raises the car using a special long aluminum jack—first one side, then the other—to allow other crew members to change tires.

2. *Tire Changers*: These experts remove the five lug nuts holding a tire to the wheel using a wrench called an air gun. They then hang a new tire and tighten the nuts. Tire changers usually work on just the front or rear tires.

3. *Tire Carriers*: These workers assist the tire changers by carrying in the new tires and removing the old ones.

4. *Gas Man*: This worker hoists 11 gallon (41.6 l) cans, one after the other, to fill the gas tank. To protect him from the dangerous fumes and fuel, he wears a special fireproof apron and helmet.

The seven pit-crew members move like a well-oiled machine to finish their jobs as quickly as possible. A good pit stop can mean a win for a race team.

5. *Catch-Can Man*: Assisting the gas man, this worker catches any overflow gasoline and helps carry the full and empty gas cans.

Pit-crew members can also deal with simple engine problems and adjust the car's setup, or the settings of its shocks, springs, and other internal parts. On some occasions, they may also need to hammer out dents, which slow down the car.

Other Help

Seven pit-crew members can go over the wall to work on the car. Other crew members have jobs to do as well. One hands the driver water or an energy drink, while another reaches out with a long pole and cleans the windshield or grill. Other helpers carry empty fuel cans, retrieve used tires, or pass tools. Another helper holds a large sign with the car's number to show the driver just where to stop. Watching it all is the crew chief, who is in charge of everyone on the race team.

TRACKS

Here's a look at the types of tracks used in NASCAR.

The first NASCAR tracks were made of hard-packed dirt or sand. Drivers spun through dusty quarter-mile (0.4 km) or half-mile (0.8 km) ovals, spinning their wheels in tight turns. In the 1950s, larger asphalt tracks were built to give drivers a better surface and provide space for fans to sit and watch the races.

Today, NASCAR runs its races on four types of tracks:

1. *Super-speedways*: These monster ovals are more than 2 miles (3.2 km) around. Drivers make all left-hand turns as they fly around the track's four corners. On opposite sides of the oval are long straightaways, as much as three-quarters of a mile (1.2 km) long. Cars reach their highest speed on these long, straight stretches. At the end of the straightaways, these turns are actually

Bristol Motor Speedway is one of NASCAR's fan favorites.

banked, or tilted. This helps the cars maintain control at high speed. NASCAR's two super-speedways are the Daytona International Speedway in Florida and Talladega in Alabama.

2. *Intermediate*: These tracks stretch from 1 mile (1.6 km) to 2 miles (3.2 km) around. Most NASCAR tracks fall into this category. They are all oval in shape, with banked turns. Intermediate ovals are located in Atlanta, California, Miami, Phoenix, North Carolina, and ten other places.

3. *Short tracks*: At less than 1 mile (1.6 km) around, these tracks make for tightly packed racing. They are more similar to the tracks on which NASCAR got its start. The small tracks mean that fans are close to the action all the way around! The small space of the tracks and the tight, banked turns mean that car wrecks are frequent. Bristol Motor Speedway in Tennessee and Martinsville Speedway in West Virginia are two of the most well-known short tracks.

The banked track at places like Daytona helps cars maintain high speeds as they race through turns.

■INSIDE STORY ▌▌▌▌▌▌

Twists and Turns

All but two of NASCAR's tracks are basically ovals of one size or another. Two others call for different driving skills. At Watkins Glen in New York and Sonoma in California, NASCAR runs on road courses. These twisting, turning tracks do not have the high banking of the big ovals. They also have more, and smaller, tighter turns, calling for better braking and more working of the gears. Some teams bring in road-course specialists to drive their cars on these courses.

RACING STRATEGIES

Racing cars is easy, right? You just put your foot on the gas and don't stop until you win! Well, there's much more to it than that.

In NASCAR's early days, being fast helped, but being tough helped more. Those were tight-packed races with much bigger cars. Cars usually got bumped and banged as they raced and traded paint.

Today's NASCAR is not so rough-and-tumble. Drivers use a lot more strategy when racing their cars. They work with the pit crew to decide when to come in for gas. Choosing when to pit, or when not to, can make a big difference in a driver's success.

Drivers are alone on the track, but they're not lonely. Their helmet radio brings reports from spotters, who are seated high above the track. Spotters report about opposing drivers' positions. The crew chief also talks to the drivers about pit strategy and about how the race is going.

One thing drivers can do to help their speed is called drafting. On the freeway, your parents would never drive at high speed, inches from another car's bumper. But on a NASCAR track, it's a regular thing. Two cars traveling that close together can move faster than each car can by itself. The car in front punches through

Drivers try to get as close as they can to their fellow racers. However, this driver got a bit too close and the side of his car was smashed in.

the air. That makes the air flow more smoothly over the rear car, which can increase speed and save gas.

The other way a driver can get the most out of his car is by learning the best line on a track. By finding the fastest and most efficient way to go through curves, the driver can keep his or her speed the highest. You'll see drivers moving up and down the track to find the best line early in a race.

This pack of cars, led by three-time champ Jimmie Johnson (48), shows how close-packed the NASCAR action can be. Each car has only a small space in which to move around.

JEFF GORDON

Jeff Gordon started out in Richard Petty's final race, and the torch was passed to a new NASCAR superstar.

As a boy in Indiana, Jeff Gordon figured that he'd grow up to race Indy cars. These are the long, sleek, open-wheel racers used in the Indy 500 and other races. The California native had moved to Indiana with his family. By the time he was six, he was winning go-kart races regularly against older kids. In fact, he won more than six hundred short-track races. At nineteen, he got his first ride in a stock car. Gordon was hooked and switched gears right away.

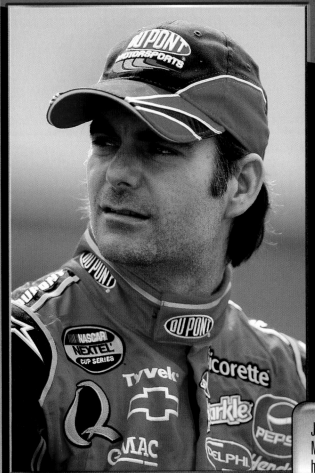

In 1991 he was the Rookie of the Year at NASCAR's second level, then called the Busch Series. He made his top-level **debut** in 1992 in the final race run by the legendary Richard Petty. By the following year he was the overall champion. He was the youngest champion since the 1950s.

Gordon was not immediately loved by NASCAR fans. They saw him as an outsider coming into their southern sport and beating their heroes. Gordon's battles with Dale Earnhardt Sr. were famous for their intensity. But Gordon's skill overcame their worries and he soon was among the favorite drivers.

Jeff Gordon had to overcome a lot to succeed in NASCAR. Not only did he have to battle other drivers on the track, he had to work hard to get fans to like him—even though he was not a good ol' boy from the south.

Here's Gordon (24) steering his Chevrolet Impala SS around a turn. His main sponsor is DuPont, a paint company, so he sports a very colorful car!

He was certainly still among the best. He won titles in 1997 and 1998 and a fourth in 2001. His four titles overall are second only to Petty and Earnhardt's seven each. He would have earned a fifth in 2006 if the Chase for the Cup had not been started. He has made the final group in the Chase every year it has been run. Gordon keeps winning races; his 82 wins through mid–2009 are the fourth-most ever. He remains among the top drivers of all time and is a threat to win every time he races.

■INSIDE STORY ||||||

Go-Kart Start

Like many NASCAR drivers, Jeff Gordon got his start racing go-karts. But, these are not the go-karts you might drive at an amusement park. Karts are a class of racing machine of their own. Low to the ground with wide, thick tires and no exterior body, karts can reach speeds nearing 60 or 70 miles per hour (97 or 113 km/h) on straightaways. Most kart courses are small and tight, so driving ability is more important than speed. Karting is more popular in Europe among adults, while in the United States the sport is more popular with young adults and teenagers.

OTHER NASCAR STARS

NASCAR is packed with top drivers. These men combine racing skill with guts and style. Let's meet a few of them.

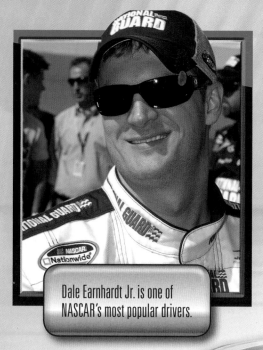

Dale Earnhardt Jr. is one of NASCAR's most popular drivers.

As the son of a legendary racer, it's no surprise that Dale Earnhardt Jr. got off to a fast start in racing. Dale Jr. began by watching his dad race, and first moved behind the wheel himself when he was seventeen. In only his second full-time season in NASCAR, he was the Busch Series champion. Moving to NASCAR's top level, he won two races as a rookie in 2000. While he has not yet won a championship at that top level, Dale Jr. is always in the hunt. He is especially good on super-speedways.

Sadly, Dale Jr. was in the 2001 Daytona race in which his dad was killed in a wreck. He later had a feud with his stepmother Theresa, who took over Dale Sr.'s racing team, for which Dale Jr. raced. In 2007 he split from the team named for his dad and joined Hendrick Motorsports. Dale Jr. is also a team owner himself. Two of his cars have won Busch Series championships.

Another top driver around Dale Jr.'s age is Matt Kenseth. Unlike most top drivers, Matt didn't grow up in the south. He was a Wisconsin native who learned to race on short tracks throughout the state and the Midwest. After joining NASCAR, he became the 2000 Rookie of the Year, and by 2003 he was the champion. Though he won only one race that year, he has had a steady stream of high finishes.

INSIDE STORY

Junior's World

Being the son of a legend gave Dale Earnhardt Jr. a leg up on fame. He has appeared on many TV talk shows. He does advertisements and promotions for many products. He even wrote a best-selling book, *Driver 8*, named for his car number at the time.

Matt Kenseth (17) surprised many racing fans when he came all the way from Wisconsin to win the 2003 title.

Two-time NASCAR champion Tony Stewart has won in just about everything on wheels. He began his career driving karts and was the world champion in 1987. He later was the first driver to win titles in three different sports-car divisions in one year. He then won a title in Indy League open-wheel racing. In 1998 he pulled off an amazing double. In May he raced in both the Indy 500 and Coca-Cola 600 on the same day! He had to take a helicopter and private plane to make it to the second starting line!

From 1999 to 2006 Stewart finished in NASCAR's top ten every year.

He was the champion in 2002 and 2005. Stewart's hard-charging style has made him popular among fans. Few drivers have had as much success in the past decade as "Tony the Tiger."

Another driver has flipped right into fans' hearts! Carl Edwards got his start in NASCAR driving pickup trucks in the Craftsman Series. Moving into cars in 2005, he finished a surprising third overall, with four victories. By 2008 he was regularly among the series leaders, challenging Jimmie Johnson right up until the end for the championship. He had an awesome year and his eight race wins were the most of the season.

Tony Stewart (20) has been a winner in whatever he drives, including earning a pair of NASCAR titles.

Fans flip for Carl Edwards' post-victory celebration as he launches skyward from his car.

Edwards is a great driver, but he is best known for what he does after he wins. Edwards climbs out of his car and stands on the window opening. After waving to the crowd, he does a backflip off the car! No. 99 is working hard to become No. 1.

Another up-and-coming driver is Clint Bowyer. In 2007 and 2008 he was part of the Chase for the Cup. Look for him to be among the leaders in the years ahead.

▌INSIDE STORY ▌▌▌▌▌▌

Busch Brothers

NASCAR is no stranger to racing families. Lee Petty and his son Richard, Ned Jarrett and his son Dale, and the Flock family, who have four siblings as drivers, were among them. The latest NASCAR family is brothers Kurt and Kyle Busch. Kurt was the champion in 2006 and remains a top driver. Younger brother Kyle came onto the circuit with a roar that same year and has been in the final top ten every season since. The former Busch Series Rookie of the Year is one of the favorites to become a NASCAR champ in the near future.

JIMMIE JOHNSON

Johnson roared to the top in 2008, winning his third straight title.

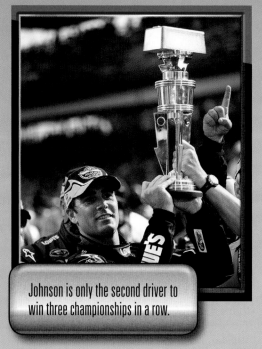

Johnson is only the second driver to win three championships in a row.

Though he is not flashy or loud, does not have a wild name or cool attitude, Jimmie Johnson does one thing really well: win. In 2008 Johnson became the first driver to win three straight titles since Cale Yarborough won three in a row in 1978.

Unlike many drivers who came from the south, Johnson grew up in California. And he didn't start out in stock cars, either, but in desert-racing trucks. Johnson bounced through desert tracks in the West and Mexico for several years, winning many races. He moved on to indoor truck racing. In these races, huge tracks with bumps and jumps are set up inside large stadiums. Johnson won three championships in this type of racing. He also won several outdoor racing titles.

He moved into sports cars in 1998 and then ran some races in the Busch Series in 2001. That's where NASCAR team owner Rick Hendrick saw Johnson's **potential** and hired him to drive in the top level. In Johnson's first full season in 2002, he won three races and finished fifth overall.

In 2003 and 2004 Johnson was second overall. In 2004 he was only eight points behind Kurt Busch, the closest points finish in NASCAR history. In a remarkable finish in 2006, Johnson zoomed ahead of several other drivers to win the Chase for the Cup and his first title. He did it again in 2007, winning four of the final ten races to grab his second title. His third title in a row came in 2008. NASCAR's latest hero follows in a long line of star drivers.

See that bump on top of Johnson's car (48)? It's part of a communications set that helps him stay in touch with his pit crew and crew chief.

■ **INSIDE STORY** ||||||

Chase for the Cup

Here are more details about the Chase for the Cup. In each race there are forty-three drivers. At the end they get points based on how they finished and for leading laps. At the end of the first twenty-six races, the top twelve drivers earn a spot in the Chase for the Cup. Their total points are reset, moving them closer together. So even if a driver has a 200-point lead after twenty-six races, at the start of the Chase, he has just a ten to fifty point lead, depending on how many race wins he had. Then they hold the final ten races. All drivers take part, but only the top twelve can earn more points toward winning the Sprint Cup.

GLOSSARY

debut   The first time someone does something.

gearheads   A nickname for people who love motor sports or cars.

intimidator   A person who causes other people to be fearful or worried.

modify   To change or make into something new.

pistons   Metal cylinders that go up and down in an engine
                   to turn the drive shaft.

potential   The positive things a person may be able to do
                   in the future.

qualifying   The race against the clock that sets the starting
                   order of a competition.

treads   The grooves on the outside of tires.

FIND OUT MORE

BOOKS

Buckley, James Jr. *Eyewitness NASCAR*. New York: DK Publishing, 2005. A photo-packed overview of everything NASCAR. See photos of NASCAR's early cars and heroes, close-ups of engine parts and driver gear, and go behind the scenes of a NASCAR garage.

Buckley, James Jr. *Speedway Superstars*. Pleasantville, NY: Readers' Digest Children's Publishing, 2004. Meet all of NASCAR's greatest drivers in this book of biographies: Richard Petty, Dale Earnhardt Sr., Cale Yarborough, Jeff Gordon, David Pearson, Tony Stewart, and many more.

Woods, Bob. *Dirt-Track Daredevils*. Chanhassen, MN: Tradition Publishing, 2004. Take a closer look at the early days of NASCAR, including stories of Bill France's early moves, the thrill of those early victories, and the road the sport took from humble roots.

WEBSITES

Visit these websites for more information:

www.lowesracing.com

This is the sponsor site of Jimmie Johnson's No. 48 car, which includes a biography of this three-time champion, as well as his teammates Jeff Gordon and Dale Earnhardt Jr.

www.nascar.com

This is the official site of NASCAR. It is packed with stats, schedules, results, video, audio, interviews, and much more.

INDEX

Allison, Bobby, 11, 15
Allison, Donnie, 11

Bonnett, Neil, 11
Bowyer, Clint, 43
Brickyard 400, 17
Bristol Motor Speedway, 34–35
Busch, Kurt, 43–44
Busch, Kyle, 43–44

Car of Tomorrow, 22–25
Craftsman Truck Series, 21

Daytona 500, 10–13, 19
Daytona Beach International
    Speedway, 7, 35

Earnhardt, Dale Jr., 40, 41
Earnhardt, Dale Sr., 13, 15–19,
    38, 41
Earnhardt, Ralph, 18
Earnhardt, Theresa, 41
Edwards, Carl, 42–43

Elliott, Bill, 15
engines, 26–27

France, Bill Sr., 6
France, Bill Jr., 6
France, Brian, 6

Gordon, Jeff, 17, 38–39
Guthrie, Janet, 11

Indianapolis Motor Speedway,
    17

Jarrett, Dale, 16, 43
Jarrett, Ned, 43
Johnson, Jimmie, 5, 11, 20, 37,
    42, 44–45

Kenseth, Matt, 30, 41
Kulwicki, Alan, 16

Labonte, Terry, 15

Martinsville Speedway, 35

Nationwide Series, 21
Nextel, 20

Pearson, David, 9, 13–14
Petty, Lee, 12
Petty, Richard, 9, 12–13, 38
pit crews, 32–33

safety gear, 30–31
Sonoma, 35
Sprint, 20
Stewart, Tony, 42

Talladega International
    Speedway, 15, 35
tires, 28–29

Waltrip, Darrell, 14–15
Watkins Glen, 35
Winston Cup, 10, 14

Yarborough, Cale, 11, 44